Visit the Zoo, vol. II

A Tom Smith Book

Electronically-Printed in the United States of America

*Frederick Fichman Publishing
7760 E. State Route 69, Ste. C5-245*

Prescott Valley, AZ 86314

fred@frederickfichman.com

Copyright, 2016

ISBN 978-1530503438

INTRODUCTION

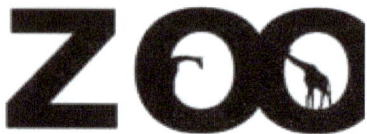

Sometimes it seems there just isn't enough time to do the fun things in life once you've discovered those things. Let's make time, how about it? Let's continue our journey in the Zoo.

Our first volume of "Visit the Zoo" was a great first look into world of wild animals. We saw all kinds of really great looking birds and mammals. But that was just the beginning. There is so much more to see. The last animal we saw in volume 1 was the giraffe. But as we look down the path we can see even more animals.

There are more sections of the zoo we haven't even come to. And sometimes it does seem there isn't enough time, like we said earlier, to see all the animals we want to see. But ya know what? Let's make the time.

That means there just has to be a second volume of "Visit the Zoo" and probably even more.

Okay, where did we leave off, oh yeah, we were looking at the Giraffe. Let's look down at our Zoo Map and let's look at the sign. Okay, what's that big area over there?

1

Lion

There he is the KING OF THE JUNGLE…stretched out, taking a nap while the lioness looks on, maybe in disgust. But ya know what, that's what lions do most of the time. They just lay around; yawning, napping, and resting…up to 20 hours a day. The rest of time is spent grooming, socializing, hunting or eating.

The Lion (Panthera Leo) is the second largest of the cat family, the Tiger is bigger. Females are smaller than males. The females can top out at 400 pounds but the males can be as big as 550 pounds. The females stand about 4 feet tall and the males 5 feet tall. But as we creep closer to the railing we can really see how big they look.

They live mainly in Africa now, other than in zoos around the world. But here is a fascinating fact: about 10,000 years ago the largest population of animals on Earth was humans. Second in number were the lions. But, sadly their numbers have shrunk along with their habitat.

Habitat is mostly on grassy plains, savannas and woodlands. You know their diet: antelope, zebra, warthog, small mammals and buffalo. One more critical point about lions, they can climb trees, so if you are walking under a tree with a lion in it ready to pounce…well, you get the picture.

Lions are very social animals and their social group, the pride, is structured with the females really the ones in charge. They have anywhere from 1-4 cubs and they live 10-14 years in the wild and about 20 years in captivity.

Either way, wild or in zoos, they are beautiful, regal, and majestic animals. They have been worshipped, feared…hated and loved over the centuries. To see one in person at the zoo is really great.

Moving on now…

Impala

Impala (Aepyceros melampus) are high on the menu list of Lions, not only Lions but also Hyena and Cheetahs. Impalas live in Africa in countries such as Kenya, Swaziland, Tanzania, Mozambique, Botswana, and Zimbabwe. Aren't those great country names? Fun to pronounce.

The live in herds that can number about 200. They like to live by the water. They are mainly grazers when it comes to eating. Their diet includes grass, shoots, foliage and seed pods. They stand about 3 feet tall and weigh on average between 88 and 130 pounds. And can they run...Wow, they have to run fast to escape predators. They can jump as far as 40 feet and as high as 10 feet. To see them run and jump and leap is like watching ballet. They are incredibly adapted creatures, born to run…to get away from the other African animals that are trying to eat them.

2

Let's look at one more nearby menu item for lions:

Thomson's Gazelle

Your probably asking right away, who is Thomson? Why was this animal named after him? Okay, here is the answer: Joseph Thomson was a Scottish Explorer who lived from 1858-1895. He was instrumental in the early European exploration of Africa. He was able to make friends or at least not anger the indigenous tribes and liked to make a "soft footprint" wherever he explored. In other words, he did not want to anger the native peoples or trash the land in his wake of exploration. This gazelle is named after him. There, now we know who Thomson is.

Thomson's Gazelle (Gazella thomsonii) is also a favorite food of lions, cheetah, African Wild Dogs and hyenas. They are

20-28 inches tall and weigh a maximum of 55 pounds for females and 66 pounds for males. They have distinctive horns, although in this picture you can see this guy has lost part of one. They live on the African savanna, mostly in the Serengeti region of Kenya.

They like to follow the Zebra and Wildebeest herds because those large animals trample the tall grasses, making it easier for Thomson's Gazelle to graze. Also fast runners sometimes up to 60 miles per hour, that's almost as fast as a car rolling down the highway. And they too like to leap or bound, called stotting or pronking. They think it startles predators. But I think the predators think, "…you're not fooling me buddy…"

Across from the Gazelles we can see a pond and in the middle of the pond a small island constructed especially for these small guys:

Spider Monkey

Moving to another nearby enclosure takes us away from Africa and to Central and South America to look at these small mammals. The Spider Monkey (Atelinae ateles) lives in the Americas in ever smaller habitat. In fact, it is considered critically endangered as deforestation occurs with the growth of human farming.

The males weigh around 24 pounds and females 21 pounds. The most interesting physical feature is their tail. It acts almost like a fifth limb, an additional arm or leg. It's about 3 feet long and allows the Spider Monkey to grasp limbs as they swing easily through the trees. Their diet is 90% fruits and nuts, making their brains a bit larger. Scientists think this is because they need larger brain capacity to remember where those fruits and nuts are so they can continually go back to find them.

They live to be about 20 years old and they are diurnal, meaning they sleep at night.

But, here is some behavior from these guys that should give you pause. When humans approach they can screech or growl. They shake nearby tree limbs and may even break one off. They don't throw it at humans but may let it drop to the ground in front of the human intruder to scare it off. But here is the disturbing behavior. Sometimes, if a human approaches they will either try to defecate or urinate on that intruder. It's best if you don't approach the Spider Monkey. You agree, yes?

3

Break Time…let's get off the trail and step inside the Gift Shop where it's cool…maybe even pick up a bottle of water.

This is a large Gift Shop in the zoo we are visiting today, but in several places in this and larger zoos there are small Gift Shops where you can always pick up a memento of your visit or hit the cooler and pick up a soda or water.

And you can even get a really cool T-Shirt, if the powers that be let you:

Back outside and on the path. In the next stop we will go inside a small building that is dedicated to the small mammal. All of these creatures are in much small enclosures that allow for the ability to control environment. Animals may require varying levels of temperature or humidity, even different light strength or time-of-day light variations can be important for the welfare of these small creatures.

Cliff Chipmunk

If you remember the old cartoon series, "Chip and Dale", that's who these guys are. They are rodents, members of the squirrel family. But, unlike their cousins the fluffy-tailed squirrels these little ones don't store fat in their bodies. And even though it doesn't look like it on this chubby guy in the picture above, instead of storing body fat they store away food. During the cold barren winter months they hit their food stocks hidden away and ready for use.

Cliff Chipmunks (Neotamias dorsalis) live mostly in the Western U.S. and Mexico. They live in cliff walls and boulder fields not far from Penyon-Juniper woodlands. They are active in the early morning and late afternoon. Of course they love to eat nuts and small fruits, even seeds. And boy are they cute, but stay away, don't touch. Like squirrels, they too can give you a nasty little bite.

4

Let's see if we can find a few more small furry creatures in the small mammal "house."

Harris Antelope Squirrel

Sometimes people will say, "…a squirrel is just a squirrel." But, not so. Sometimes behavior is so strange you have to pay a bit more attention. Now, this squirrel pictured above is called a Harris Antelope Squirrel (Amospermophilus horrissii.) First of all look at that scientific name, pretty cool, hunh? But, the really cool fact? Hold on.

This squirrel lives primarily in the western and central part of Arizona, in a portion of New Mexico and in or near Sonora, Mexico. They eat fruit, seeds, mesquite beans, insects and even an occasional mouse or two. Their predators are coyotes, hawks, snakes and household cats and dogs. They live 2-4 years, weight 4-5 ounces, they are 8-10 long; their tails are 3-4 inches long.

Okay, here are the two really cool parts. They are active in the middle of the day, even when it is really really hot. They will run around like crazy until they over heat and will use their tail as an umbrella to shade their heads. Then, when they get overheated they will perform a "heat-dumping "maneuver. They find a shady spot and then they lay flat on their stomachs, arms and legs out-stretched, spread-eagled as the saying goes, and will lay there on their tummies until they cool down.

They guy pictured above was jumping around and then suddenly found a cuddly spot in the rocks, curled up in a ball, head down, and just sat there, "chillin." One thing you can say about these guys, they sure know how to take it easy.

Okay, let's take a look at one more little creature before we leave the Small Mammal Building. All these little mammals are so cute.

Red-Handed Tamarin

Well, this tiny fella does not look happy, does he? He is called a Red-Handed Tamarin **(Saguinos midas.)** His hands do look more yellow than red, it must be because of the artificial light.

The reason he doesn't look happy may very well be because of where he lives in the wild. Tamarins live in the Amazon River Basin, South America. They live in countries like Brazil, Guyana, French Guiana, Suriname…in the jungle. Their families usually have 4-15 members and they are naturally aggressive and spend a lot of their time defending their territory. The families are dominated by a single female and the juveniles are taken care of by the father.

They are wonderful climbers and can leap from tree to tree in distances of over 60 feet. Their bodies are between 8 and

11 inches long and they are lightweight little dudes weighing only one pound at the most. Their tales are 12-17 inches long.

These Tamarinds eat protein, they are meat eaters. They eat small insects, small animals, lizards, spiders and frogs. But trying to eat them are Birds of Prey like Eagles and Hawks, Cats and Snakes. So, it is understandable why they are aggressive and mean-looking. Just look at the picture of them above and you'll see.

Alright, bye little guy, see ya. Moving on.

5

Speaking of frogs, let's slip inside for a quick look at the Amphibian Building.

Colorado River Toad

This is another one of these animals you might see in the zoo that can be nominated for a "YIKES" designation. The Colorado River Toad (Bufo alvarius) is nasty.

First of all, they are big. They are 7.5 inches long, and except for the Cane Toad, which is a non-native U.S. toad, it is the largest toad in the United States. But that is what not what makes this thing scary. Look carefully at the bumps along its side in the picture above. See them? Those are not just ugly warts, those bumps contain a potent toxin, or poison, that can kill even a grown large dog…and they have.

Raccoons and other mammals know to stay away from these creatures. They live in the Arizona, New Mexico and Mexico region of the world and prefer semi-aquatic habitat but can live in desert as well. They are carnivorous. This means they eat meat or other animals. They like to eat insects, rodents and other small reptiles. They are nocturnal and like to move around at night. They communicate with a loud piercing call.

If you see these fellas or hear them, stay away. Don't touch.

Here is another beauty in the Amphibian Building.

Pancake Tortoise

Have you ever heard of the old saying, "Flat as a Pancake?" Well it applies to this tortoise. The Pancake Tortoise (Malacochersus tornieri) is called the Pancake Tortoise because it is flat. And it is flat because it needs to be if it wants to hide in the crevices between rocks. Seems logical. But the carapace, or shell, is also porous and they can become easy prey if they are not careful.

It grows to be about six inches long and likes to eat succulent plants and shrubs, those plants are juicy and sweet. But they also like dry grasses as well. They eat those plants in their native homes in east Africa, mainly Kenya and Tanzania. They make their homes on rocky outcroppings and hillsides from elevations of 100 to 6,000 feet.

They are fast and agile climbers and are active early in morning and in the early evening. The rest of the time they eat and rest. They take life at a slow pace and lazily eat their food and go about their minimal exploring.

6

    As with vol.1 in this series, let's end this edition of "Visit the Zoo" at the point where we started, with our cover "Beauty" shot. This time let's walk over to the Meerkat enclosure, everyone's favorite.

Slender-Tailed Meerkat

These precious mammals have received a great deal of worldwide attention over the years because they are so cute. They are fun to watch as they watch us when we approach their open enclosure. They stand erect and proud and always vigilant. And from the look of the Meerkat above, they like to eat as well.

Meerkats are members of the Mongoose family but they behave and act much like the North American Prairie Dog. They live in Africa in the Kalahari Desert in Botswana and in the Namib Desert in Namibia. They burrow into the ground in colonies or clans with about 20 members. They live to be about 6-7 years old in the wild or 12-14 years in captivity.

Both males and females weigh about 1.6 pounds. They have wonderful binocular vision with good peripheral vision, they can see to the sides very well.

Among colony members there is a great deal of sharing of duties for either gathering food, raising young, or making improvements to their underground homes. Several individuals in the clan are designated as lookouts. As with the Meerkat pictured above, they are on alert all the time, looking skyward for the dreaded Bird of Prey eager to dive down on them and snatch them for a meal.

The Meerkats eat insects, eggs, rodents, and birds. They have a wide and varied diet.

There is one behavior that our photographer was able to catch which is rare and rarely seen. The picture below was taken early on a cool morning at the zoo in the Meerkat enclosure. Approaching these two Meerkats you would think something horrible had happened to them, were they dead? No, as you can see they were just laid out flat on their backs, sunning themselves, trying to get warm. It is this type of universal cuteness that makes them endearing all around the world.

SUMMARY

Well, unfortunately that is all we can see and describe in this volume of "Visit the Zoo." And again, we have so much more to see and talk about. We haven't come yet to the leopards or bears or tigers or any of the aquarium fish. But that is coming in following volumes. So, join us again as we "Visit the Zoo."

THE AUTHOR

FREDERICK FICHMAN is the author of this series. He lives in the southwest United States and is crazy about animals and travel and photography. He has dozens more books ahead.

Be sure to check out Volume 1 of "Visit the Zoo"

END

www.ingramcontent.com/pod-product-compliance
Lightning Source LLC
Chambersburg PA
CBHW050925290526
45792CB00002B/894